If You're Happy

If you're happy and you know it,
clap your hands.

If you're happy and you know it,
clap your hands.

If you're happy and you know it,
then you'll surely want to show it.

If you're happy and you know it,
clap your hands.

If you're happy and you know it,
stamp your feet.

If you're happy and you know it,
stamp your feet.

If you're happy and you know it,
then you'll surely want to show it.

If you're happy and you know it,
stamp your feet.

If you're happy and you know it,
say "Ha! Ha!"

If you're happy and you know it,
say "Ha! Ha!"

If you're happy and you know it,
then you'll surely want to show it.

If you're happy and you know it,
say "Ha! Ha!"

If you're happy and you know it,
do all three.

If you're happy and you know it,
do all three.

If you're happy and you know it,
then you'll surely want to show it.
If you're happy and you know it,
do all three.